LOG HOUSES
Classics of the North

LOG HOUSES
CLASSICS OF THE NORTH

PHOTOGRAPHY BY
PETER CHRISTOPHER

TEXT BY
RICHARD SKINULIS

National Library of Canada Cataloguing in Publication

Christopher, Peter
Log houses : classics of the north
photographs by Peter Christopher ; text by Richard Skinulis.

Originally published under title: Log houses : Canadian classics.

ISBN 1-55046-389-6

1. Log cabins — Canada.   2. Log cabins — Canada — Pictorial works.
3. Log cabins — Design and construction.   I. Skinulis, Richard, 1947-   II. Title.

NA8470.C48 2003   728'.37'0971   C2002-905399-4

Publisher Cataloging-in-Publication Data (U.S.) is available.

A BOSTON MILLS PRESS BOOK

Published by
BOSTON MILLS PRESS
132 Main Street
Erin, Ontario, N0B 1T0
Tel. (519) 833-2407
Fax (519) 833-2195
books@bostonmillspress.com
www.bostonmillspress.com

IN CANADA: IN THE UNITED STATES:
Distributed by Firefly Books Ltd.   Distributed by Firefly Books (U.S.) Inc.
3680 Victoria Park Avenue   P.O. Box 1338, Ellicott Station
Toronto, Ontario M2H 3K1   Buffalo, New York 14205

The publisher acknowledges the financial support of the Government of Canada
through the Book Publishing Industry Development Program (BPIDP) for its publishing efforts.

Design by Gillian Stead
Printed in Hong Kong by Book Art Inc.,Toronto

To our fathers,
builders in their own right

*Each year, the owners of this reconstructed log homestead stage an elaborate old-fashioned Christmas
that includes a sleigh ride and three Christmas trees.*

CONTENTS

This log home overlooking the Pacific has been a family retreat for generations.

PREFACE

At the heart of this book is the desire to celebrate a truly timeless tradition as well as a truly unique craft. The handmade log home is a symbol of the rugged spirit and survival mentality of the pioneers who settled this land. They didn't have much, so they used what they found, often with great skill. The log home was the wooden equivalent of the Inuit igloo or the Bedouin goatskin tent. No matter how sophisticated or modern they have become, the log home is still a place to shelter from the long, cold nights.

A lot has changed since those early pioneering days. For instance, the phrase "hewers of wood" — once used to describe an honorable occupation — has become a derogatory term for North America's reliance on a natural-resource-based economy. In answer to that, we looked for the best examples we could find to show the level of beauty and craftsmanship that hewers of wood — both past and present — can really accomplish. We wanted to inspire would-be builders and owners, and anyone else with dreams of living in a home made of "big wood," to dream big dreams.

Finally, photographer Peter Christopher and I felt a book like this was necessary to document the renaissance of a style of building that seemed only a few years away from becoming a lost art. Back in the early 1970s, a small group of novice log-builders caught the tail end of a generation that still remembered how to hew a log smooth and push it onto a wall. To this pool of knowledge was added a willingness to experiment and learn from trial and error. The result appears on these pages.

Although I am not a log builder, I have for decades had an interest in any building constructed from the big wood. I have owned them, lived in them, written about them and even helped build a few. I've driven the back roads looking for old log buildings to buy and spent countless hours talking with old-timers about their experiences building and living in log structures. Once

This gazebo perched on an outcropping of the ancient granite is part of a vacation hideaway in the woods.

immersed in the mystique of the log home, it is hard to shake the attraction. If you have any kind of historical bent to your nature, that interest is compounded.

To find homes for this book, we talked to log builders and log-home owners across North America, always asking the questions: Why did you build a log home? What does it mean to you? What's it like living in one? They responded by talking to us, feeding us, letting us sleep in their homes, and by taking us to every other log building in their area.

You can't build a wooden structure in most North American cities, so we found most of our homes in those scenic wonderlands where people go to get away from the speed and grit of urban life. Log homes tend to be located in clusters — in the Pacific Northwest; in the rugged woodlands of the Northeast; in the ski and vacation areas of the continent's mountain ranges. Log builders all know each other. I spent two years being passed from builder to builder, each knowing of at least one spectacular log building that simply had to be included in the book. We tried to follow every lead in order to provide examples of only the very best log homes.

The classic Eastern loggie: practical, conservative and architecturally pious. This is a historically accurate reconstruction, even to the window sizes. Replacement logs came from two hewn barns.

The bedrooms of this loggie have built-in bunks. Their large size makes them well suited to the monolithic proportions of a log home.

While the builders had a lot in common, the owners were a surprisingly diverse group. If I have learned one thing on this project, it is that everyone — from young urban professionals to retired blue-collar couples to European business tycoons to rusticating hermits — can be caught up in the dream of owning a cabin in the woods. Of course, some of the "cabins" are 5,000-square-foot luxury homes, but they all share a link to the past and very humble beginnings.

Log building is an ancient art with constantly evolving styles and improvements. There are five main methods of building with logs: hand-hewn, with dovetail corners; long-log (or Scandinavian scribe); stackwall (or cordwood); French-influenced piece-on-piece; and vertical log (or stockade). We have tried to depict as many aspects of these different styles and their refinements as possible. We have also chosen to use only those log homes that have been handcrafted. Although there is nothing wrong with the many excellent pre-manufactured kit homes on the market, the idea of every log being machined to identical size and shape does not fit with our view of the log-building tradition. Handcrafted log homes are true to the history and image of the classic northern log home. The age of mass

A rather elaborate stackwall storage shed.

*Furnishing with antiques is a natural choice for most log-home owners. It was easy for this owner to decorate —
he owns an antique store that specializes in Russian antiques. These logs were peeled by schoolchildren using peeling spuds
(small, sharp shovels), and the inside was finished in water-soluble wax.*

marketing and industrial duplication is the antithesis of what the northern log home stands for — rugged individuality and patient craft — and log-home owners and builders themselves tend to go slightly against the grain of our mechanized society. In other words, they stand out.

This book could not have been completed without the help and encouragement of many fine log-builders, as well as the people they built the homes for. Most of the owners have chosen to remain anonymous, but we wish to thank these builders in particular: Ed Campbell of Ed Campbell Log Homes Ltd., one of the fathers of modern log-building; Doug Lukian of Lukian Structures and Design Inc., who not only made some beautiful log homes himself but also found Lac Echo for us; Ian McKay, president of Pioneer Logs Ltd.; Louis Hansen of Hansen Handcrafted Log and Timber Homes; Peter Hutley of Hutley Log Homes; Cliff Walker of Timbersmith Log Construction Ltd.; Brent McIvor of Ultimate Log Homes; Tony Jenkins; Rob Varey of L.C.&B. Construction; Tim Davies of Hammond and Davies Log Building Ltd.; and Duncan Morris of Traditional Log Homes Ltd.

A log home nestled in the woods and covered with a thick blanket of snow. The northern dream.

THE ALLURE OF THE BIG WOOD 1

Close your eyes and think about the early northern settlers. Nine times out of ten the first image that comes to mind is a log cabin, blanketed in snow, with a promising wisp of smoke rising from the chimney. Perhaps the most amazing aspect of log homes is not that people built them long ago, but that people are still choosing to build and live in them.

To live in a log house is to return to the simple pleasures of the past, surrounded by all things natural. The log home is the summation of the rural good life, even to those who live in the city. It's like living in a painting by Krieghoff. The rustic northern dream home.

No matter how modern the look or high-tech the materials, each log home carries within it at least some element of its beginnings. The log-home tradition began, of course, with the pioneers who gathered building materials to build from the resources that they found around them in the wilderness. People used rock and stone to build enduring fireplaces and foundations. They gathered moss for insulation and animal skins for blankets. But mostly they used trees. Pioneering would have been a different story without trees. Early settlers heated with wood and shingled their homes with bark. But most important, they were able to construct sturdy houses quickly by using the inevitable byproduct of clearing the land — logs.

In terms of construction, logs are a perfectly bioengineered product. A single tree can provide insulation as well as interior and exterior walls, all in one neat package. This had distinct advantages for the settlers: They didn't have to haul logs to the mill and expend money and energy to shape and trim the wood, nor use expensive nails, and then find something to use for insulation. All they had to do was cut the trees down and stack them up. We northerners have built absolutely every kind of structure out of logs, from Russian Orthodox churches — complete with onion domes — to schools, icehouses and even mausoleums. We have made them with the bark off and with the bark on, round, square, and even octagonal.

Those who chopped down the trees for a living also lived in buildings made of logs. In Canada and parts of the northern U.S., men who worked in the bush weren't always referred to as lumberjacks, but were more often called shantymen, after the combination bunk- and cook-house called a camboose shanty (from the French *cambuse de chantier* — *cambuse* meaning "provision room" and *chantier* meaning "lumberyard"). The camboose shanty was as rough-hewn a log building as ever existed, often topped with a sod roof or even a scooped roof (made from hollow logs or bark strips laid alternately face up and face down and interlocked like Spanish tiles). The camboose was made to go up fast and be disposable.

Most log homes were made to last longer. Even though log-building methods have shown a marked tendency to cross-pollinate, different ethnic groups each had their own style of building with logs, and they brought these with them when they came to the New World. The Germans, with their history of fine cabinetmaking, specialized in nicely hewn buildings with precise dovetail corners. The Irish seemed to favor this style as well, while the Scandinavians were experts in the long-log style, with its saddle-notch corners that stick out at the ends like toy Lincoln Logs. The post-and-beam frame building method was used by both English and French colonists. Sometimes called timber-frame, post-and-beam uses big squared-off timbers to make a sturdy frame that is then filled in with anything from sawn boards to stones and bricks. Often the space between the timbers is plastered over, with just the outside of the frame showing. The French called this style *colombage* and were the first in North America to use logs to fill in the spaces between the timbers, either vertical, angled or horizontal. This last came to be called piece-on- piece, from the French, meaning "bit by bit," and is explained along with vertical-log in chapter 4.

No matter what the style, log homes from the seventeenth to the nineteenth century evolved from the early jerry-built shelters to good, solid homes in their own right. They were not, as many people now think, a stop-gap solution until a real home could be built, but perfectly respectable places to live.

It wasn't until the beginning of the twentieth century that the log home began to fall out of favor with a populace obsessed with being modern. The invention of the mass-produced nail and the mass-produced brick brought what we think of today as normal housing within the grasp of most segments of society. Log homes became not only unnecessary but something to be ashamed of.

A cluster of modern log homes in Whistler, British Columbia. Although firmly rooted in the past, these buildings —
vacation properties built in a scenic location, using different building styles and even tinted exterior finishes —
have many of the distinctive characteristics of today's log homes.

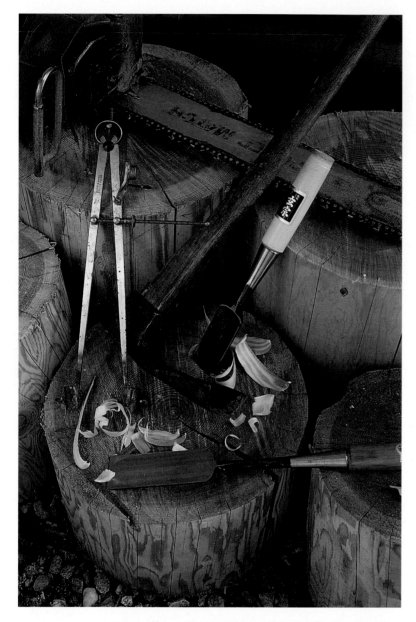

Virtually any log building can be built using these four basic tools: a chainsaw for shaping and cutting; an adze for hewing logs flat; big chisels called "slicks" for finishing joints; and a set of scribes for tracing the contours of the bottom of one log onto the top of the log below it.

They were covered up, torn down and sometimes even burned to the ground, the better to retrieve the nails, which did have value. It seemed the link with the past that log homes provided was a little too close for comfort. Although some truly amazing vacation lodges and hotels were built using logs, notably in upstate New York and in Quebec at the Château Montebello hotel, by the beginning of this century a rough-and-ready hunt camp or outbuilding was considered the only proper use for a log building. The reputation of the log home continued to slide until the craft was in real danger of dying out.

Happily, log-building is enjoying a renaissance these days. The rejuvenation of the art of building with the big wood began in the 1970s with the back-to-the-land movement when young urban people — including the author — began moving to the country. Those who joined the migration caught the last breath of the log-building tradition. They bought land that had old log barns and original log homesteads on it. Sometimes they just wanted inexpensive yet unusual homes for themselves and saw the opportunity of buying used cabins from local people, who were only too happy to sell buildings they considered second-rate.

Fascinated by these icons of the past, the newcomers soon began delving into the local log-building history. Log homes and outbuildings were everywhere, as were the people who had lived in them and a few who still called home. Each building had a history and someone who could tell you about it. It was not unusual to buy an old log home from someone who had grown up in it or even helped move it to its new location (despite their size, log buildings are highly portable).

Surprisingly, there were almost no books on log construction back then. What there was consisted of the reminiscences of these old-timers, as was noted down by the new, young builders before all first-hand knowledge of this arcane craft was lost. They spent hours listening to elderly local people talk about putting up the buildings in their youth. In the seventies, when a log building was going up, a local expert would often be standing by, sagely explaining how to push and pull the logs up on greased poles.

There was a great supply of hewn logs and not much demand during the sixties and early seventies. This economic situation changed considerably during the mid-seventies. For a few years you could acquire a set of logs either very cheaply or for absolutely nothing. To the people who had grown up beside abandoned log buildings, these structures had no worth. But as the knowledge of log-building grew, with every new builder willing to learn by trial and error, the number of people who could turn out a well-made building increased. They learned from the old-timers and were taught by others who had recently learned the craft and set up schools. By the late seventies, people began building cottages and luxury homes out of logs, often in high-priced areas near big cities. It was not uncommon for two or three old loggies (the term "loggie" is a diminutive used by builders) to be put together to form a single dwelling. As the price of a set of antique logs rose, this new wave of builders began to buy new logs and build loggies from scratch.

Today's log builders have raised the craft to a degree that rivals that achieved in its heyday. Sure, modern handcrafters use chainsaws to rough-cut notches before finishing them with hammer and chisel, and logs are increasingly milled to uniform sizes before being hewn, but the growth and exchange of information between modern builders has resulted in extremely high standards. A flood of books on the subject, and log-building schools and organizations, have spread ideas and techniques further than our ancestors could ever have imagined.

This new boom in log building has brought with it a stimulating cross-fertilization. The long-log Scandinavian full-scribe style with saddle-notch corners that used to be found mostly in the

Note the French-influenced bell-curve roof on this loggie. Even the taste for exuberant coloring is beginning to spread within a construction style that was formerly conservative.

Pacific Northwest can be found just about anywhere now. The square-hewn building style of the Northeast, with its precisely made dovetail corners, is just as likely to be found in the Northwest. And, to the dismay of traditionalists, exuberant West Coast conceits such as fancy timbered gable-ends and colorful milk-paint stains are beginning to appear on some otherwise dignified Eastern structures. Hewn buildings are now designed with soaring cathedral ceilings, something not seen even thirty years ago. And the found-art style that employs naturally growing curved trees as banisters and railings is also making a comeback. We are even beginning to see different styles melded into one house. For example, one wall will be hewn flat and the other three left round, a style that works because logs are the most forgiving and malleable of building materials. This adaptable nature also means that different log homes can be fitted with different architectural features — Georgian doors and side windows on one, Victorian scrollwork on another — and still look like everyone's idea of a log house. Even the piece-on-piece style that, along with the distinctive bell-curve roof (see page 22), goes back to the beginnings of French-colonized Quebec in the early seventeenth century, has grown past its borders.

Meanwhile, a new and completely external influence has appeared on the log-building scene. The Japanese, by their seemingly inexhaustible fascination with all that exemplifies what is wild and expansive about North America, have become the world's largest export market for handcrafted log homes. For instance, Japanese importers account for 85 percent of the almost one thousand log buildings that Canada exports every year (about 44 percent of the total number made in Canada). But they have not been so passive as to merely buy. The woodcrafters of Japan have a long history of extremely fine quality joinery. The Japanese buyers of log homes have passed on this demand for high quality to their North American suppliers. The result — apart from an increase in work for log builders — has been to make our log-building industry the best in the world. It's what one West Coast builder calls "the best thing that ever happened to the log-home industry."

Not that North American log builders needed much encouragement. The builders we have run across — as well as the customers they build for — have shown a rare respect for what they make and for the raw materials they use. They will also go to any lengths to build a log house in just the right spot, whether at the top of an almost inaccessible mountain peak (see page 60)

A covered entranceway leads to stairs that descend to the log house itself. This charming structure shows how versatile logs can be. The family wanted a presence on their cul-de-sac, but also wanted to turn their back to the roadway and maintain as much of their privacy as possible. This unique logwork structure satisfied both desires.

or on a Pacific island (see page 8). They make barges, lay miles of underground pipes and wires, and build roads through impossible terrain. They are the kind of people who will build a 20-ton timber-frame bridge over an existing 5-ton bridge in order to bring the logs onto a building site. They make sure they plant more trees than they use. Often they use horses to skid the logs out of the bush, an expensive and time-consuming method that nevertheless avoids the war-zone look created by clear-cutting. And they can go to even greater lengths. In one case, the owner and builder collaborated, at great expense in time and money, to use a crane to lift every log of a new home over a few mature trees instead of bulldozing them down. To them it was natural. "We had to save those trees," explained the builder. "After all, we're in the tree business."

Fancy timbered gable-ends such as this were once found only on Scandinavian-style buildings. These days, almost anything goes.

Cool in the summer and warm in the winter, this hand-hewn log home is brand-new but looks as if it grew here a hundred years ago. The actual logwork was done at the builder's lot and then the logs were brought to this site to be re-erected. By the time a building is completed, each log may be moved as many as seventeen times.

THE HEWN-LOG HOUSE
The Perfection of the Dovetail Corner

2

Drive along any back road in the eastern United States or central Canada and eventually you will come upon a hand-hewn log house. You can't miss them. The distinctive honey-gold of pine or the silver-gray of eastern cedar logs, outlined with long lines of white chinking, seems to rise out of the landscape as if they grew there — which, in a sense, they did. Add spiky rows of cedar shakes and a fieldstone foundation and you have the classic square-hewn loggie, whether it is a hundred-year-old homestead or a brand-new home fresh off the builder's lot.

The hewn-log house has two defining characteristics: the sides are hewn square by hand, and the corners are joined together by dovetail joints. This kind of house is, as log reconstruction expert Tony Jenkins says, "the arrowback chair of architecture — everyone recognizes them as being old, as being an antique style."

The logs were hewn flat to resemble a "proper" house, and to make interior paneling easier. Some in fact were hewn so flat and chinked so tightly on the inside that when whitewashed they looked like plastered walls. Hewing also has the happy effect of cutting off the outer layer, or sap wood, which is where most of the shrinkage occurs, leaving only the more durable heartwood. Another reason for hewing is that a round log's shape tends to let the water run onto the log below it, while flat-hewn logs shed the water easier.

Beyond looking good, the dovetail corner has an almost perfect functionality. Preferred by German and Irish settlers (Scandinavians favored the round saddle-notch corner), it's the ultimate wood joint; interlocking, self-draining and immensely strong, "dovetail" has even become a verb for something fitting snugly together. Visually pleasing, a well-made corner of dovetails rising up evenly to meet the eaves represents order, craftsmanship and a rare precision. This love of the dovetail corner is also the main reason you almost never see corner windows in a loggie.

A beautiful example of a modern log home. The dovetail corners and perfect chinking are accentuated by a gray stain. This Rocky Mountain vacation home has a Japanese dripchain that channels water from the eavestrough to a drain in the ground.

Along with these practical matters, what the best examples of the hewn home have in common is a certain organic quality. No matter how grandiose or urbane, to truly work architecturally, a log house has to retain some link to its humble past. It has to look as if it belongs in a rural setting. As one builder put it, "A log house should look like it grew right up out of the ground."

To achieve this, attention to detail is a must. This starts with the front of the house. You can put in all the sliding-glass doors, skylights and hot tubs you want, as long as you keep the front looking traditional. Keep the logs low to the ground and avoid any indecent flash of concrete block between the sill (lowest) log and the ground. We don't want to even *mention* walk-out basements. And no matter how convenient aluminum windowframes may be, we've never seen any that look good on a log house.

For the log "cabin" look (builders hate this rather pejorative term, by the way), a single story is fine, but the traditional hewn-log home should be comprised of one and a half stories. The half-story "knee wall" on the second floor can be made of log or frame, as both were used. This not only generally looks better than a two-story home, but the one and

a half stories make the most practical use of space as well. A steep roof-pitch, all the better to shed the heavy northern snow-load, is also considered traditional — perhaps with a ten-to-twelve or twelve-to-twelve rise over run, or approximately a 45-degree angle.

Ideally, the front of the house should not be visible from the road. This reinforces the concept of the log home as a retreat, somewhere tucked away and sheltered from the bumptious glare of the world. For this reason, many designers and owners insist on underground service lines and they add at least one dogleg to the driveway.

Running water, rock, and trees tinged with autumn color: Log homes tend to be built where there is a view of nature at her most wild and beautiful.

A porch on a hewn building cuts down on the interior light, but it does add another dimension to a vacation home. This builder has added an unusual twist by slightly extending the dovetail corners.

The idea of a front porch is also contentious. Scandinavian-style long-log homes seem to accept porches better, and you see a lot of them out west, where there are bigger vistas to be enjoyed from a rocking chair. Although there are many exceptions, the Eastern hewn house did not traditionally have a big porch, if any at all, because a porch tends to cut off the light. Besides, a porch is only good for sitting on, and the early settlers were a pious, hard-working lot who had little time for non-productive activities. The French added some flair with their bell-curved roofs, and the Scandinavians did the same with their chalet-style balconies and fancy exposed beamwork. But dour old Ontario log homes, with their functional size, unadorned style and stingy, prim-looking roof overhangs, had God-fearing conservatism written all over them. Today, of course, you can build whatever you want as long as it is within the bounds of architectural good taste, even a porch on which to muse the hours away in non-productive bliss.

Window size is another area where most people are willing to give a little. Historically, windows in loggies were small, especially in those houses thrown up quickly on the frontier. Windows let the heat out. And real glass was so expensive that pioneers resorted

A good log home minimizes the division between the inside and the outside, as is accomplished by the large number of windows here.

This distinctly non-traditional log home was designed to let in as much light as possible. The soaring, glassed-in cathedral ceiling and broad surfaces of light-reflecting interior drywall add to the effect. One interesting part of this building's story is that every log was lifted by crane over three red pines in order to save them.

to substitutes such as greased paper and even rows of empty pickle jars. But the ready availability of thermopane and present-day preferences for building on scenic sites have resulted in some rather huge picture-windows in otherwise traditional loggies. On the bigger buildings this even seems to work, probably because it fits into the larger scale of building and building material.

This home was built to house the owner's mother's antique collection. (The previous owner of the harvest table was reportedly killed by his son as they ate dinner at this table.) The comfortable jumble of old couches and curios, along with the requisite stone fireplace, make this a classic interior. The low windows to the right make this a perfect spot for long muses over a cup of tea.

The roof is a domain where innovation is suspect. For example, if possible, eavestroughs should be made of wood, not plastic or metal (two flat pieces joining to form a simple V will do). Asphalt shingles and tin roofing are fine for other rural buildings, but the first choice among log aficionados has to be the funky good looks of cedar shakes. If you split them yourself, especially from trees grown on your own property, so much the better. We know one owner who used to offer visitors a drink, but with the proviso that they take up a mallet and a sharp axe and split off twenty or so shakes from an 18-inch log. It took fifteen years to finish his home, but he glows with pride over every shake on that roof. Homemade shakes are not tapered like the manufactured variety and therefore look a little bristly, but also more authentic.

A solid-looking stone chimney bolstering one side of a log wall is also traditional. (Some early log cabins even had a log chimney, called a "slave cabin" chimney.) And any log home worth its salt should have a fireplace. If you can cook on it — maybe with a pot suspended over the fire — so much the better. A crackling fire in a stone or rough brick fireplace does more than provide heat; it evokes the past *and* makes a great replacement for the ubiquitous television.

Interlocking, self-draining and immensely strong, the dovetail corner has an almost perfect functionality.

Some of the numbers painted on to help in reconstructing this Blue Mountain ski chalet are still visible. One log is charred as a result of the fire used to burn off the bark.

One place where adherence to early tradition is not desirable is in the gable ends. Back when it was hard to get sawn boards, many people extended the log courses up to include the gables. This can still look all right with the long-log style, but is strictly overkill with a hewn building. Stick to boards, V-groove siding, or board-and-batten.

Matters of style aside, it is the very fact that a hewn-log house has been visibly worked that makes it special. A large part of its charm is contained in the axe marks of the woodworker — marks that can go back centuries. You are surrounded by reminders that someone has actually *worked* this wood. The thousands of chips, grooves and cuts give the logs a lived-in texture and a visible, tactile history that makes this style of building unique, especially if it is a reconstruction of an old building.

Mind you, this rough-and-tumble appearance is exaggerated when a building has been dismantled prior to reconstruction. Many an owner has reeled in shock when the logging truck has dropped the newly purchased building — which looked great when standing in its original location — into a pile at the new site. Nothing is less impressive than a pile of old logs, especially ones that may easily have cost $10,000 to $20,000. With pieces of strapping,

One look at the stingy roof overhang tells you this house is in Ontario.

This house is composed of the original log homestead, built in 1860, and a frame addition from 1920 sheathed in barnboard from the original barn. Restoring this loggie was a lot of work. This home was originally built with a dirt floor, and when reconstruction began a few years ago the front wall was buckled out 9 inches. Floor joists were rehewn for use as replacement logs, but because they were of red cedar, they had to be specially stained to match the existing pine logs.

chinking and other hunks of wood hanging off the logs, broken dowels sticking out, broken logs, logs with pieces of rot showing, and logs with sections charred black from fire, your potential new home doesn't look as if it would make good kindling. At this point it's the builder's job to calm the owner and restore confidence in what is starting to look like a hopeless project. Fortunately all it usually takes is a couple of courses of logs going up to make the sun shine again. That said, the possibility of buying a pig in a poke (a truly bad set of logs) is always there, and buyers should check out a dealer's reputation carefully. Ask your region's Log Builders' Association for a list of its members.

A planting of day lilies hides the foundation of this century-old hewn loggie. Note the ends of the second-floor beams that come right through the wall.

Darkly stained logs and pure-white chinking make the logs stand out in sharp relief. This particular builder's signature is found in the tall, pointed finial that runs through the top of the roof peak, as well as the medieval European-style timber trusses that frame the gable ends. Present-day log builders add distinctive elaborations to their designs.

If you do have a pile of logs waiting to be re-erected, make sure they don't lie on the ground for more than a week. Rain can seep into cracks and crevices, creating rot, and mould thrives on logs that are touching wet ground. Just because your logs survived for a century doesn't mean that they're invulnerable. They survived that long because they were kept relatively dry and off the ground.

To make discolored, painted or white-washed logs look better, the logs can be sandblasted, which cleans up the logs beautifully but leaves them a little soft and porous. Water and chlorine in a one-to-one solution will remove mildew, and a high-pressure water treatment can be also be used to get rid of stains. Some hardy souls even grind off the outside layer with sanders or mechanized wire-brushes. The process is just like stripping an old pine chair, only about a hundred times more work. But then the resulting satisfaction is correspondingly greater.

These are all fairly recent innovations that go hand in glove with the present high value placed on antique logs. But as we have mentioned, it wasn't that long ago that original handcrafted log homes and outbuildings were available cheap, or even for the asking. In fact, log homes went out of style as early as the

Log buildings are the original mobile homes. In 1943 the cedar cabin section (on the left) of this ski chalet was moved from northern Ontario to the top of the Niagara Escarpment, and then moved again twelve years later to its present location on Blue Mountain. In 1960 the black-ash logs for the right side of the building were hauled in by hand from a few miles away.

Each of these logs was turned periodically over the course of a year so that the inside would be the same color gray as the outside. They make a fine backdrop for primitive handmade furniture.

turn of the century. They may have been considered acceptable for a rustic cottage or hunt-camp getaway, but anyone who still had one as their primary residence did everything they could to camouflage the offending logwork. The fine workmanship of farmers and their neighbors was covered up with sheets of Insulbrick, board-and-batten, and even courses of concrete block. When log homes became valuable again in the mid-seventies, log builders drove the back roads and small towns looking for the telltale signs of extra-deep window wells of up to two feet in thickness that told of hidden treasure behind the aluminum siding. As recently as fifteen years ago, many farmers would let you have a log building just for taking it away and filling in the hole. News that some of these giveaways were being resold for thousands of dollars pushed the price up. Today, this mother lode of vintage log buildings has been almost used up by dealers, who did everything from placing ads in local papers to renting planes to fly over the backwoods looking for abandoned farms.

If you are lucky enough to find an old loggie today, the first thing to do is to check for rot,

The mantelpiece of this fireplace is made from a ceiling beam from an old hotel. The mortise hole on the right is a handy place to put matches.

A very successful adaptation of a 170-year-old log homestead with two modern additions by two prominent architects,
Ron Thom and Seymour Seligman. The owners wanted to expand but didn't want a reproduction, so they decided simply
to go with something that looked good. The result is two modern, vaguely Japanese additions built ten years apart
that do indeed look good, mainly because the construction materials tie the buildings together visually.
The log cabin is one of the few old loggies we have seen that is still on its original site.

especially in the bottom tier of logs that sometimes rested on the ground and in those under the windows. Pounding on the logs with a rubber mallet is a good way of detecting hollow spots caused by rot. But even if there are rotten logs, they can be replaced.

Taking down an old loggie can be done by hand (if you have enough hands available) with low-tech tools as simple as planks for sliding the logs down on, ropes for slowing the descent, and cant hooks for manhandling them. But be careful; these big tree-trunks can be quite brittle after sitting in a wall for a century or two and can break if dropped. Better to use a logging truck with a cantilevered claw, which can take the logs on or off its flatbed and put them

One of the modern additions to the original log homestead. The architect decided to not try to compete with the loggie, but used building techniques and natural materials, such as elaborate timber-trusses, stone floors and cedar shakes, to tie the two together.

A stone wall relieves the tedium that can result from too much wood and seamlessly ties an old log home to a modern addition.

43

The logs for this music-room addition to an existing log home came from a storage shed that was once a church. The large, arched window on the left wall is an element of the building's previous incarnation, as is the loft that once held the choir. The owners got around the problem of finding a place in a loggie for light switches and wiring by having only lamps. The wires come up through the floor.

anywhere you want. Hydraulic cranes are also used. During construction, the pros usually construct scaffolding around the building. And the wooden pegs that were used to hold the top two or three courses of logs together have to be cut (modern builders generally use threaded rod instead of wooden pegs).

Most log homes were small one- or two-room affairs with internal walls made of frame. But if you are *very* lucky, you will find one with internal walls made of logs. Sometimes a particularly wide home will have an internal wall running the width of the building and keyed in to each side wall for added strength. This is a rarity and worth a greater expenditure. We have always liked the look of internal log walls from the *inside*, but the necessary joints that show on the outside tend to break up the clean lines of the log wall. The choice is yours.

A lot of reconstructed log-homes are made from pieces of different structures. It's not uncommon to see logs from four or five different homes, barns and outbuildings making up one home. The ability to adapt and recycle makes log construction the most malleable and forgiving of building methods. It's not unusual to see old ring-bolts, hand-forged nail-heads and pieces of wire sticking out of a wall or ceiling beam in an otherwise impeccably appointed luxury home. Because

The honey-gold of old pine boards — some as wide as 25 inches — provides a rich backdrop for the antiques that decorate this chalet. The floorboards were originally nailed right through but are now toe-nailed on an angle so that the nails don't show.

The chunks of wood at the lower right are called spacers and were used to hold the logs up while they were being nailed into the window or door frame. The most forgiving of buildings, log homes make a virtue out of these practical necessities, and owners tend to put them on display instead of hiding them.

these building were often moved, the lucky log-owner may proudly point out the old Roman numerals cut into the logs near the corners for the original builders so that they would know which logs went where (today's builders use stamped, galvanized-steel tags). We have seen everything carved on old logs, from people's names to euchre scores. These historical touches add greatly to the charm of a log home.

Taking down these old structures can be an adventure. Bats, wasp nests, hysterical starlings and flying squirrels protecting their nests — all leave signs of their presence on the logs and are routinely pointed out to visitors.

The history of the building can also be revealed. We were puzzled by the division apparent in the floorboards in one original homestead built in in 1861. They indicated that the building had at one time been divided. We later found out that this was done by a brother and sister who had each been willed half the house by their parents. They actually split the rather small log-cabin into two separate homes, one with eight layers of wallpaper, the other Spartan and plain. It's also fun, when dismantling an old loggie, to find the ancient newspapers used for insulation in the walls or ceilings. They not only provide distraction from the work of deconstruction, but also give us a sense of time and place for the original inhabitants.

Also found in reconstructions are the spacers, chunks of wood wedged in between the courses near

Old signs and antiques fill this drive shed attached to an old log home in the Laurentians.

door and window frames to keep the logs separated before nailing them into the frames. In any other building method, these structural anomalies would be hidden. Here, they are a big part of the charm of log homes (see home on page 46). Instead of being hidden or removed, they are lovingly pointed out by proud owners.

This respect for the history of a building and the logs that make it up knows no bounds. The meandering paths of wood-eating insects grooved into the wood are usually considered blemishes, but since a loggie serves so well to record the myriad of tiny events that have happened to it during its long life, all such signs merely add to the home's charm. Builders look for these little pieces of found art embedded or embodied in the wood: a dramatically curved tree is brought back to the yard to be used as a handrail on a staircase (see photo on page 108); gouges made by the

With a right angle every 26 feet, this home of canoeing enthusiasts has lots of interior dovetails showing. It costs more money, but it's nice to have these examples of exceptional wood-joinery on display inside.

sharpening of a deer's antlers are conspicuously placed in a wall over a dining-room table (see photo on page 106).

Logs were, and still are, hewn square on two sides with a tool called an adze (though a modern innovation is to cut them flat at the sawmill and then put the hewing marks on last). An adze has a sharp axe-like blade set at right angles to the handle so that the worker can whittle the surface of the wood while standing over it.

It is a mistake to think that loggies were merely a stepping stone to a frame or brick residence. The fact is, they were fine-looking houses, and very warm and tight once you worked enough oakum (horsehair or hemp impregnated with tar) into the chinks and plastered them over with mortar — a process called chinking.

Chinking is a laborious task. It takes time to do well and is damn cold on the hands if done at any time other than summer. But modern technology comes to the rescue again, this time with new products such as the popular PermaChink, an acrylic chinking compound that adheres to the wood as it expands and contracts with the change of seasons.

The main idea of chinking is to make the water drain off and to keep moisture from

Contrary to popular opinion, log homes were not just stepping stones to a real house, but perfectly acceptable homes in their own right. Often they had paneling nailed to strapping, as in this authentic reconstruction. Note the Georgian fan-window over the door. Concealed within the antique armoire in the corner are a modern stereo and television.

The ski trails of Whistler, British Columbia, give the owners of this stunning home the kind of view loggies were meant to have.

seeping into the wood. This is a vitally important aspect of hewn-log construction. As much as a log building is sealed, the chinking is what seals it. For that reason, it is important to have the bottom of the top log overhang the log below it in what is known as a drip ledge. The chinking is run up underneath this overhang, and the seal where it meets the log is thus protected from the weather. It takes practice to get the hang of troweling plaster between the logs so that it looks smooth and provides a good seal. But don't worry; if you don't use one of the modern, plastic chinking compounds, you'll get plenty of practice.

In the old days, mud and straw, and even manure and straw, were used for chinking, especially on barns and outbuildings. You were likely to find just about anything stuffed in behind the mortar, from oakum to moss, newspaper, chunks of wood, and even stones. These materials (except for the stones) were used for insulation and to give the mortar something to grab onto. Today, the inside of the chinks are often stuffed with fiberglass or expandable foam insulation, covered by a plastic vapor-barrier and then chicken wire or wire-mesh plasterer's lath. Chinking may not be fun, but those spaces between the logs provide definition to the logs and, more practically, give you a place to put things like electrical wires and plumbing.

The hewn-log home is considered relatively high maintenance. The chinking has to be done and redone over the years, and water has to be prevented from sitting anywhere on the logs. The extra work that hewing entails and the precision it takes to make a good dovetail add up to more time and expense than other log-building methods. Still, the hewn-log home is a beauty to behold and, to many of us, the epitome of the log-builder's art.

The sheer immensity of round logs cries out for huge vistas, tall mountains and big skies.

THE LONG-LOG HOME

3

The Art of the Scandinavian Scribe

While hewn-log homes are neat and well-defined, buildings made of round logs rise up robust and strong. The bulging effect of the logs, with their stabilizing and protruding ends, conveys the feeling that they could withstand anything — storm, seige or flood. The long-log home is a fortress that makes no excuses. Logs are big and round? So be it. This is a building style that doesn't try to improve on Mother Nature.

The technique of building with long, or round, logs comes from Scandinavia. There are two ways of building with long logs: easy and not quite so easy.

The easy way is to rough out a saddle-notch corner and drop one log on top of another. There is no need to hew the logs flat, and in the old days, they sometimes didn't even peel them. The gaps between the logs were chinked just as in a square-log building (some people disparagingly call modern buildings built this way "chinkers"). They were a little drafty, but they went up fast.

Today we use a little more finesse, as well as some interesting tools. The result is a chinkless wall so tight and sculpted that, as one builder says, "It looks like the logs are eating each other."

First the bark is peeled off the logs. There are two ways to do this. If the log has been cut in the spring, when the running sap creates a layer of moisture between the bark and the wood, you can peel the bark off by splitting it down one side (using a short-bladed shovel called a peeling spud) and pulling it off like a giant cinnamon stick. Peeling a dry, winter-cut log is harder and usually involves scraping the bark off with a drawknife (essentially a long blade with a handle at each end, normally used for shaping wood). Drawknifing is an exceedingly tedious job, but fortunately there are professional log-peelers, most of them in the Pacific Northwest. They use custom-made drawknives that are precisely shaped and sharpened. This attention to detail pays off, in that a good peeler can strip a 30-foot log in forty minutes or less.

A log staircase framed by log walls provides a medley of shapes — straight and angled lines, plus the pleasing roundness of the logs themselves. One of the reasons this method of construction is so labor-intensive is that each log is drawknifed smooth to remove the bark. The logs were finished with transparent Swedish oil.

The peeling results in a smooth finish to the logs, while drawknifing gives it a hewn, worked look. Some people even like to leave a little of the bark on, though leaving all the bark encourages insects. The logs can theoretically be any kind of softwood (hardwood such as oak or maple is too heavy, not rot-resistant enough, and doesn't have the insulation quality), including the so-called junk trees such as spruce and fir. But by far the favorite choice is red and white cedar (cedar has the best rot- and disease-resistance qualities), followed by pine and then by fir (which can have a spiral grain, giving it what some builders call a mind of its own). Softwood is easier to work, and because it has more tiny air compartments, it is a good insulator. In fact, one inch of Western red cedar has an R (resistance to heat transference) value of 1.56, just about half that of fiberglass insulation. One point in the long-log method's favor is that you don't have to hew off any wood, which means the log will be thicker and therefore have a higher R value.

The main criteria in choosing logs is that they be straight, not have too many limbs that form knots, and be between 18 and 24 inches in diameter at the butt end, tapering down to

The outside of this home is proof that a well-designed loggie will look good anywhere, even if it is not traditional in style. At an extra cost of $5,000, two cranes were used to hoist the logs over existing trees in order to minimize damage to the environment. It may seem an extravagance to some, but this kind of care is typical of many log-home owners.

no less than 16 inches at the narrow end (this is an average, with Western logs being bigger than the Eastern variety). The taper of the logs is alternated as they go up, to ensure that every log is as level as possible. Each wall-log averages 30 to 45 feet in length and will cost between $150 and $200 wholesale. Keep in mind, however, that many perfectly good cabins and cottages are made with much smaller and cheaper logs, often using lesser varieties such as spruce and balsam. If you're lucky, you can cut them yourself on the site, or offer to clear some land for a neighbor.

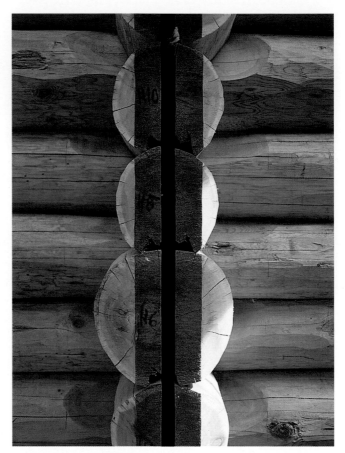

The round-log method uses scribes to trace the contours of the bottom of the top log onto the top of the log below it. The line is then rough-cut with a chainsaw to make the saddle-notch corner pictured here. The same method is used to make each of the wall logs fit snugly.

A groove is cut by chainsaw into the log ends of a window or door frame. A wooden spline that is attached to the log ends is then inserted into the groove so that the logs can slide down as the building shrinks and settles.

It takes about forty logs to build an average four-corner home. Most builders either own woodlots or have a deal with a lumber company that will let them walk their lots and mark the trees they want. Because a handcrafted log home is, by definition, custom-made, the average cost will range from $100 to $150 a square foot — substantially more than the average frame or even brick equivalent.

Once the logs are cut and peeled, the long-log method next involves the use of scribes — essentially an overgrown set of dividers. The scribes used in the early days were rudimentary and consisted of just two pointed metal arms joined at one end. Modern scribes often have attachments for pencils and even built-in bubble levels. The scribes are used to copy the contours of the bottom of one log onto the top of another. This undulating line is then cut with a chainsaw. Doing it right is an art in itself, but when cut by an experienced builder, the logs seem to melt into each other. The reason for this complicated working of the wood is to snug the logs up tight and eliminate the need for chinking. Still, insulation is often stuffed into a V-groove cut out of the bottom of the log, and caulking is sometimes used to seal the logs where they meet.

The V-groove between the logs is a good place to run the plumbing and wiring. A common challenge with all log buildings is deciding where to run your services. With frame walls this is so easy it's hardly thought of at all, but with log homes and their solid walls, it takes ingenuity and constant fore-thought. Chimneys can double as places to run heating ducts, but there are other services that are harder to mask. Take the electrical

The inside of this ski chalet is heated with a remarkably efficient "old-tech" fireplace that also acts as a room divider. It is of North European origin but made by a company in Port Colborne, Ontario, and faced with Fox Island granite (Fox Island is just off the Sunshine Coast of British Columbia). Inside is an 8,000-pound mass of channels, buffers, flues and heat-exchangers that serve to burn and reheat all of the resulting gases. Twenty-four hours after the fire goes out, the masonry still gives off heat.

Posts of Douglas fir that soar up to support a high ceiling in a design by architect Bernd Hermanski evoke the big trees of an old-growth forest. The southwestern flavor was inspired by the owner's former home in Arizona. The architect managed to make use of a lot of glass but not too much; overdoing the glass can reduce the building to a glorified log window-frame instead of a true log home.

Where log-building used to be fairly simple, modern engineering coupled with Old World craft allows builders to produce some incredibly intricate beam- and log-work. This example manages to create a sense of massiveness and delicacy at the same time.

plug box — where do you put it? Between the logs? On top of the logs? Some industrious builders even hollow out a space right in the log to set the box flush with the wall. And more than one home has an electrical cable running as unobtrusively as possible along an exposed beam before disappearing into a wall. And floor plugs are common in log homes because it is so easy to run the wiring under the floorboards.

For this and other reasons, logwork takes a great deal of forethought and prep work. Most of the basic logwork is done at a builder's yard, where the shell of the building is made to a customer's specifications, first by roughing out the notches with a chainsaw, and then doing the finishing work with chisels, axe heads, and slicks; a slick is essentially a giant chisel with a long metal handle. The shell, complete with window and door openings, is then taken down and trucked (or barged — a surprising number of loggies are built on islands) to the owner's site, where it is reassembled and the finishing is done. In total, each log may be moved from one place to another (including on and off the wall when fitting a joint) as many as seventeen times.

No expense was spared with this loggie, tucked in the woods 350 yards above Lake Okanagan. The roof is made of cedar shakes, the eavestroughs and gutters are handmade from wood, and the fittings are custom-built wrought iron. To preserve the view, the deck walls were made of glass in a post-and-beam frame. The water, electricity and telephone lines were laid under a 165-yard-long switchback driveway — all to preserve the natural beauty of the hilltop.

The bird-motif designs cut out of the deck posts were created by West Coast carver Bill Wyett.

BELOW LEFT:
Detail of wooded eavestrough and pipe. Notice how the saddle-notch corners in the background flow into each other in a distinctive, solid kind of beauty.

Doing it this way, instead of bringing the logs to the construction site, has a few advantages. One is that the builder's yard is close to his home and the homes of his crew, while the customer's site is usually off on some hard-to-get-to lake or bush road. The other advantage is that logs are by their very nature big, clumsy, heavy, and more than a little dangerous. Log buildings are almost megalithic. Each log weighs hundreds of pounds and can be as big as 28 inches in diameter and 40 feet long. Log builders need all the engineering help — lifts, pulleys and cranes — they can get, all of which they have at their building yards. You have to be in shape for this kind of work — it's not like moving plywood or even bricks around. And chainsaws are a lot

Builders like to bring back an interesting tree or branch from the bush. This nicely finished, forked trunk holds up a ceiling joist. Notice the mortise-and-tenon joint that joins them.

The curving shape of this old-fashioned bathtub complements the aesthetics of a round-log home.

heavier than hammers. To be efficient, log builders need the physical conditioning of athletes. They become phenomenally adept at moving these big blocks of wood around; an experienced builder can coax a ponderous log into virtually spinning on its axis with only a simple crowbar or cant hook (an oversized baseball-bat-shaped wooden handle with a hinged hook at one end). They also have to stay alert, because when mistakes are made with the big wood, they are usually big mistakes. One log builder put it this way: "If a carpenter makes a mistake on a two-by-six he can recut it. Make a mistake on a log joint and you're out four hundred dollars."

With its Hudson Bay blankets and quilt, this bedroom achieves a Spartan elegance. Notice the short interior log wall at the left. Although expensive, structural touches such as this one make log homes fascinating to look at and live in. One question, however: How did they get the wire to that lightbulb on the underside of the ceiling joist?

Round logs invite architectural extravagance: elaborate rooflines, decks, overhangs — all on a larger-than-life scale.
This West Coast home constructed of tinted wood fits the bill.

Lots of glass, stone, and big, round beams help this log home achieve its main purpose — to relieve stress. It's the feeling of space, along with the soothing effect of big, round wood, that contributes to the feeling of relaxation that a log home provides — which is why many vacation homes and getaways are built this way. A crackling fire adds to the effect.

Speaking of mistakes, one of the scarier aspects of long-log construction is the shrinkage factor. Although there is no shrinkage through the length, a long-log wall will shrink, on average, 4 to 6 inches through its width (a hewn-log wall is mostly shrink-resistant heartwood and will shrink 2 inches at most). About 90 percent of this shrinkage will occur in the first two years. To accommodate this, various ways of allowing the roof to settle over the windows and doors have been perfected by log builders over the years (for details, see chapter 6).

The best way to minimize this shrinkage is to build with dry, seasoned logs. Some builders will dry their logs for up to three years. One builder even likes to leave the shell, including the roof, on the site for at least six months whenever possible to let the building settle and dry out even more. Actually, the best place for logs to dry is in the wall, as long as the process is a slow one. If green logs are used in a house, with the heat from a furnace drying it out fast, expect some rather large checking to appear, along with some dramatic shrinkage.

Resembling one of those truly remarkable log lodges in upstate New York, Yellowstone Park, and Canada's Château Montebello, this family "cottage" is an example of how far from the pioneer cabin we have come.

Log buildings are essentially modular, and although most work crews are small in number, a building can be constructed very quickly if there are enough skilled workers involved. Perhaps the most spectacular example of this is in Canada — it's definitely the biggest — at Château Montebello. About 40 miles southeast of Ottawa, the Château used to be a private club (the Seigneury Club) and is now a Canadian Pacific hotel. It was built in 1930 by over 3,500 skilled craftsmen from Quebec and Scandinavia in an astonishing two months. Think of it — 10,000 Western red cedar logs all hand-scribed to fit, and done in less time than it takes to build an ordinary house. Built in an era when log buildings were supposedly on the way out, Château Montebello still stands as a challenge to today's log builders now that this historic and bigger-than-life style is enjoying a renaissance.

The use of big logs seems to encourage a flair and even an extravagance in the design of modern homes. Huge roofs, extended overhangs, exaggerated Gothic dormers, large windows and big, big logs all play a part. While square-log buildings are often nestled in the woods, long-log homes are more likely found cantilevered over a sheer drop-off, or surrounded by huge vistas, expanses of water or golf courses. You are also more likely to find the elaborate beams and carved posts of cathedral ceilings in long-log homes, as well as complicated gable-ends with the same kind of fancy beamwork. In some new homes, 20- and 30-foot

The thin cross-hatching effect of the short rafters under this skylight is an effective counterpoint to the round mass of the ceiling beam. More and more builders and architects are loosening up when designing log homes, resulting in innovative touches such as this.

Although they used to be found right across the continent, even in early towns and cities, log homes are found today only in rural areas where people go to live the rural life, or at least to get away from the clamor of city life for a few weeks.

Another example of the soothing nature of big, round logs. The warm, honeyed tone of the reflected light fills the room with a mellow glow.

interior posts soar up to the eaves. If hewn-log homes are steeped in traditional feelings of solidity, long-log design fires the imagination and revels in the dramatic.

It's probably the sheer size of the round logs that makes this dramatic flair possible. Nothing is hewn off them, and the slow curve of the wood conveys a strong feeling of size and bulk that seems to spread to everything else — furniture, setting — and especially the architecture. This last aspect is very important because the architecture of long-log design is based on proportion. It is essentially a massive medium and, in terms of design, not for the timid. Often the logs are bigger at the bottom — as big as 28 inches around — and become gradually smaller as they go up the wall. This should not be consciously noticeable, but is used to subtly offset the heavy proportions of the roof. A big roof-overhang with massive roof purlins (roof beams used to support rafters) will look good with an equally massive porch or entranceway. Gothic dormers also work well with a big roofline. Get the proportions right and it will look good and stay that way for centuries. But put too small a roof on it, for example, and it ends up looking like a man wearing a hat that's too small for his head.

One of the hallmarks of the long-log method (also known as round log, or Scandinavian scribe) are log ends that protrude from the wall, often cut in the shape of a curve. This roof offers a good look at the massive purlins (beams that hold up the rafters) used in log construction. Note the flowerpots made from hollowed-out tree trunks.

Modern appliances such as refrigerators tend to look out of place in log interiors. This owner solved the problem by cladding his fridge in solid wood. The woodstove to the left is a modern reproduction.

This support beam was carved to resemble a totem pole — an appropriate detail for this West Coast home.

For all of these reasons, the trimwork is usually large and often complex. As with some aspects of Victorian design, log homes need heavy trim. Multiple trim with sometimes three or four pieces built up to make a baseboard or trim off a window is used; even staircases and banisters are made with big wood. Staircases are often angled forward slightly and hinged at the top so that they can settle into their proper plane as the logs shrink and settle. Another method is to place blocks that can be knocked out later under the bottom. In keeping with the adaptable nature of log homes, none of these methods is meant to be hidden; they are incorporated in the design, thus turning a functional oddity into an intriguing design feature and conversation piece. (See photo on page 101.)

Comfortable wicker furniture, a glass of white wine and a sunny day in the mountains — paradise, log-home style.

There is also much that can be done with the butt ends, the two or three feet of log that protrudes out past the saddle notches. Some builders alternate these ends in and out a few inches or even feet, creating a zigzag effect (called a "Flintstone corner" by at least one builder). Others bevel or carve the ends, or have the ends get longer as they get closer to the ground (or vice versa) in a curving effect that is very Scandinavian. We have even seen the ends painted, sometimes one color, sometimes a riot of color that gives the house the playful vibrancy of a Gypsy caravan. This is not to every log-builder's taste, however. We were sternly lectured by one expert who says you should never paint the butt ends. "Look at the ends on a rainy day," he explained. "They will be wet. That's because the log is moving the water out through the same tubes used to transport water from the roots to the leaves. Painting them blocks their flow."

As for the color of the logs themselves, there are two schools of thought: natural and preserved. The natural camp likes to let the sun's ultraviolet rays turn the logs gray by killing a paper-thin outside layer of wood — which is exactly what will happen in time unless you do something to prevent it — and *then* putting on some kind of sealer. One log-builder splashes saltwater on pieces of trim and even whole logs for customers who like the weathered, ancient look. The other school likes to put some kind of finish on the logs, particularly the outside. We have heard dozens of theories of what should and should not be put on a log. Some builders swear by a mixture of linseed oil and turpentine; others buy commercial penetrating stains such as Sikkens, sometimes containing a slight tint, for the outside, and use a clear lacquer on the inside. Both methods are supposed to keep the logs from growing grey and also protect against rot and insects. Various varnishes are also used. The history of log building records people who have painted logs, burned the outside surfaces to preserve them, and even used coatings of toxic substances like creosote. The recent interest in color and the bursting of the traditional bounds of log-building have led to increased experimentation with coatings and pigmented stains, usually

The long, chunky stone steps leading up to this log vacation home fit the proportions needed for a home made out of the "big wood." Stone makes excellent landscaping sense, as do local shrubs such as juniper and white pine. The average size of the logs in this home is 16 inches, but the largest used is 26 inches around. The outside was finished with a Sikkens stain, and a clear lacquer finish was used on the inside.

A hexagonal drive-shed. Logs lend themselves to almost any shape — round, square, octagonal, whatever. Depending on the building method, a log wall can be sent off at any angle you want.

oil-based but also some new latex-based stains. A builder in the Pacific Northwest who only uses Western red cedar because of its natural beauty regularly grinds off the top inch or so to clean up the wood, and then puts on a clear sealer with just a hint of tint to block the graying effect of the sun. Others spray on different mixtures of pigmented stains. Builders have tried throwing into a clear sealer everything from chainsaw oil to MinWax (the chemical reaction from the latter method reportedly achieves some beautiful old-fashioned color). The recipes for different tints and looks are jealously guarded secrets among builders.

Whatever the color, the long-log method offers a feeling of massive solidity, along with a beautiful flow of line, that makes it one of the most popular methods of building with logs.

Massive purlins and a fieldstone walkout basement provide a firm visual foundation for this round-log home.

A well-built example of the vertical or stockade style of log building. The short length of wall-log means that one or two people can build with this method using material that wouldn't be good enough for a conventional log building. That makes this style perfect for isolated cottages and hunt camps. This home overlooking Lake Erie is made of white spruce.

OFF THE BEATEN TRACK 4

In some ways, the humble wooden log is the perfect building material. It grows wild, it's easy to prepare (just fell it, limb it and cut it to length), it's strong enough to hold up a roof and keep out the elements, yet soft enough to be easily cut and shaped. Moreover, it contains its own insulation and doesn't have to be painted every few years.

Another asset is its flexibility — there are any number of ways to take a pile of logs and make them into a house. Sometimes it makes sense not to go with the traditional method of interlacing long, straight logs with notches at the corners. This Lincoln Log approach is fine if you have the money, the manpower and the material. If you don't, or if you would just rather take the path less traveled, there are some interesting alternatives, including stackwall, piece-on-piece, and vertical-log building.

The legend of the vertical-log (or stockade-style) building, at least of the kind you find in the North, goes something like this: In 1954, veteran trapper, prospector and builder Mickey Clement was busy one day trying to mouseproof a log building he was putting up. He ran a chainsaw he was fixing along a log a couple of times, and then slid a scrap of plywood into the groove. It fit perfectly. What Clement had done was invent (or, more likely, reinvent) the spline-and-groove method of stockade-style log building.

The spline is a piece of plywood 2 1/4 inches wide and as long as the wall log. Each vertical wall-log has two 1-inch-deep grooves cut into the log about 1 3/4 inches apart. The plywood splines form a double weather-seal, and insulation is packed into the space between them, along with plumbing and wiring.

One advantage of vertical-log construction is that when the logs shrink sideways — about a quarter of an inch — the shrinkage is easily absorbed by the splines. This method also sheds water better than horizontal logs. But the clincher is that anyone handy with a hammer and chainsaw

In the stockade style, the vertical logs are joined with plywood splines that run between them. Although dried over the winter, these logs shrunk a quarter of an inch over their width. The shrinkage was easily accommodated by the splines. The logs have had the bark drawknifed off, but some was left on to give them a rustic look. The outside was finished with linseed oil and turpentine.

The burls (knotty tree-growths) on this black spruce porch-post give an interesting appearance to this stockade-style home. The builder told us that if you find a burl on one tree, you will almost certainly find more in the same location.

can build a vertical-log building virtually anywhere there are trees, making it the perfect choice for a wilderness cabin.

If you fly into a hunting or fishing camp in the bush of northern Canada, chances are you will be staying in a stockade log cabin. The reason is, nobody is going to fly in building materials to an isolated lake or mountainside, but they will fly in a one- or two-man crew. There is always wood available, and it's not a problem if it's scrubby and twisted, because this low-tech method thrives on adversity. The logs used for the walls are only 8 feet long, so trees that wouldn't be suitable for

A big house made out of the big wood needs big rooflines to maintain a sense of proportion. The high peaks on this roof keep the building from looking too squat.

Constructed in one of the oldest log building-styles, this piece-on-piece building was originally a Hudson's Bay Company post before it was moved south to serve as a garage. Unlike most modern piece-on-piece structures, this one has a post-and-beam frame that is square, not round.

more mainstream log construction because of bends or knots can still be used for the stockade style. This relatively short log-length means that two people, or even one person, can put up a building without having to use heavy equipment. The gable ends can also be made of logs, laid either vertically or horizontally.

There are builders who live for this kind of job. They fly in on a float plane to some picturesque and totally isolated lake with nothing but chainsaws, hammers and nails, and some food. Almost everything, from the walls and gable ends to the doors and cedar shakes, can be harvested from the surrounding bush. After a few weeks of quiet work, with nothing but the loons to break the silence, it must be satisfying to stand back and behold a structure truly carved out of the woods.

This sense of satisfaction goes back a long way. Vertical-log builder Rob Varey, who has researched the subject, claims it could be the oldest log-building method there is. The earliest buildings were probably no more elaborate than logs with their ends buried in a trench to form the walls. Examples of this archaic method still exist in the form of stave churches built around A.D. 950 in Norway. The trench was eventually replaced by a wooden sill-log, with the vertical wall-logs joined to it by a mortise-and-tenon joint. The stockade style came to North America in 1670 when the Hudson's Bay Company built its first trading post this way at Rupert House in the Northwest Territories (Rupert's Land at the time). Later on they were used for bunkhouses in logging camps. Although it's rare to see this method used for a principal residence, there is no particular reason not to.

Most of the other fringe methods of building with logs involve a post-and-beam frame that is filled with logs in some way. It could be vertical logs in a stockade style; vertical and angled logs in the French *colombage* style; short logs the width of the wall, mortared into place with the ends showing (stackwall); or horizontal logs.

Built in the French-influenced piece-on-piece style, this home is a good example of how this chunky style encourages builders to set walls flaring off at different angles.

Piece-on-piece involves building a post-and-beam frame and then filling in the spaces with short filler logs laid horizontally.

This last method is called piece-on-piece (also Red River, or Manitoba frame, by some people in western Canada). Its advantages are similar to those of the stockade style in that the pieces used are shorter than the more traditional styles — generally only 8 feet long — and therefore lighter and cheaper logs can be used. However, people also build piece-on-piece with big, chunky logs for a truly massive look. This style is modular, so different teams can work on different sections at the same time. You can also extend the walls off at any angle you choose, which means some interestingly shaped buildings can be made relatively easily. In fact, most hexagonal or octagonal log buildings are piece-on-piece.

Built by West Coast woodcarver Bill Wyett and his wife, Wendy, this cedar piece-on-piece home was created almost entirely out of the bush that surrounds it. Almost nothing was thrown away; even the curtains were made of woven cedar strips. Because the longest wall-log is only 8 feet long, the big crews and lifting equipment more conventional log-building styles need aren't required for this building style. Zen-like in its attention to detail, the upstairs of the Wyetts' guest cottage is aglow with beautifully shaped and finished wood.

Bill Wyett finds much of his inspiration in Native culture, Japanese influences, and nature. This delicately carved facia-board shows traces of all three sources.

Swooping falcons form the inspiration for this fluid design.

The horizontal filler-logs are scribed and cut to fit each other just as in the Scandinavian-scribed (or long-log) method. There are different ways to join these horizontal logs to the vertical posts, including V-shaped notches and plywood splines. The posts and beams that make up the frame these filler logs fit into can be round — the look most modern builders seem to like — or hewn square. Some beautiful examples of the square-hewn approach, which has French roots, can be seen in the reconstructed fortress of Louisbourg, on Cape Breton Island.

Where piece-on-piece uses logs that aren't quite good enough for the hewn- or long-log methods, the stackwall technique uses everything else. With this method, short pieces of logs are mortared in, side-by-side like bricks, with the ends of the logs showing. This creates almost total flexibility, both in materials used and in building shape. As far as the wood goes, if you can use it for firewood, you can use it for stackwall. Perhaps that's where this technique gets its other name — cordwood construction. These short, round logs can fill in a post-and-beam frame (almost always cut square), or be used freehand to build a round building or any other shape desired (see the pictures on pages 86 and 87).

Stackwall doesn't have the classic lines of horizontal-log homes or the comforting feeling of bulk that the bigger logs give to a building. But the log

These roof beams appear to be "floating" in the mortar-and-log wall.

This charmingly eccentric stackwall home is round, a shape made possible by the unlimited scope of this construction style. The retired couple who built this home had no previous building experience. They chose stackwall because it is inexpensive (almost any kind of wood can be used) and there are no heavy logs to lift. When their grandchildren misbehave, the owners threaten to make them count all the logs in the wall.

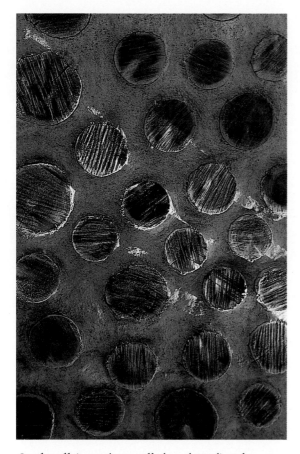

Stackwall (sometimes called cordwood) style simply uses firewood-size logs set in mortar. This kind of wall is extremely fire-resistant and has the added ability to move moisture from areas of high humidity to areas of low humidity. This last reason makes it particularly popular for animal barns. Because the logs expand and contract while the mortar that surrounds it does not, homes for human habitation are usually built with a double log wall with insulation and a vapor barrier in-between.

ends, with their interesting growth-ring patterns and differences in coloring, make a nice wall when set off by a white mortar background. And stackwall is the most fire-resistant of all log-building methods.

Despite these advantages, there are very few stackwall homes. If you see a stackwall building it is usually a barn or other outbuilding. There's a good reason for that. Logs placed with their ends exposed are very efficient at transmitting water vapor from areas of high humidity to areas of low humidity, making them a healthy choice for animal barns. For that reason, many barns are barnboard on the top, where hay is stored, but stackwall on the bottom, where the animals live.

If used in a residence, however, a double log wall is needed if there is to be any hope of keeping the drafts out. It's the same old problem: Logs shrink and expand but mortar doesn't. That means that there is always going to be some kind of space opening up around each and every log. You could caulk every seam, but that's rather unattractive and is of dubious practicality. For human habitation a double wall is a must. This means building a wall of logs and mortar, then a vapor barrier (usually a plastic sheet), followed by an air space that can be left open or filled with insulation, and then another wall of logs and mortar. This is time-consuming, but every method has its drawbacks. Stackwall might not sound like much, but it is a cheap way to go and it's definitely not something you see every day.

One of the distinctive log cottages of Lac Echo in Quebec. A collaboration between three local artisans created this uniquely charming pocket of old-time log buildings.

THE LOG COTTAGES OF LAC ECHO 5

Back in the 1940s, when rich Montrealers wanted to get away from it all, they drove north for an hour into the Laurentians. Rolling, thickly wooded mountains surround hundreds of lakes. This is cottage country, made famous by novelist Mordecai Richler, whose character Duddy Kravitz dreamed of buying land around one of these very lakes near Ste. Agathe. It is also one of those pockets in rural Canada that contains a rich vein of log buildings.

On one picturesque lake, Lac Echo, a man named George Binns began buying lakefront lots and building simple, rustic log cabins out of the local spruce and balsam just after the Second World War. A local builder and carver, Walter DaRold, built the fieldstone chimneys and contributed decorative carvings around doors and mantels. This serendipitous coming together of diverse talents was made complete when transplanted artist Helmut Gransow began adding old-fashioned European designs to walls, ceilings, shutters and even furniture. The result is an utterly charming community, an enclave of homes that all have a common theme but that are nonetheless individually distinctive.

Lac Echo was originally the summer home of families who would arrive the day school was out and not go back (except for commuting fathers) until Labor Day. This way of life took root in a slower, more gracious era. The lake has seen some changes over the years. In the early days the owners were predominantly from the Anglo middle class. In the mid-fifties it was a retreat for many McGill University professors and their families; they crisscrossed the lake in the small two-seater paddleboats that Lac Echo is famous for. These days the heads of some of Canada's wealthiest corporations unwind here on weekends, surrounded by the handiwork of three original craftsmen.

The cottages are all very similar: long, thin logs with saddle-notch corners that are caulked at the seams and painted with a dark brown walnut oil-based paint inside and out, or have turned dark brown with continuous coats of varnish or linseed oil. The smoky-brown background, the

In the late 1940s and early 1950s, a local builder named George Binns began buying lots on the lake. He cut down the local spruce and balsam and built snug little cottages of pleasing proportions. Local craftsman Walter DaRold built the stone fireplaces and carved the wood, inside and out. When landscape artist Helmut Gransow began painting the walls, shutters and even the furniture, the cottages of Lac Echo became unique.

A typical Lac Echo interior. Walter DaRold carved the mantelpiece to look like rough bark, one of his specialties. He also made powerful, rustic furniture, such as the three-legged stool in the middle of the room.

many carved posts, doorways and beams, and the designs painted on walls, ceilings and furniture, combine to create an atmosphere that can be darkly rococo. The thirty or so cottages that circle Lac Echo are pleasing in their proportions; they fit in well with their surroundings on the slopes leading down to the lake.

As the area became more exclusive, wealthier people from Montreal began buying up the cottages and adding on to them. Red-shaked roofs began to appear, along with sunrooms and terraces. Some of the larger cottages have grand galleries on the second floor that look down on living rooms centered around big Walter DaRold fireplaces. Low stone walls mellowed with green moss line the long, meandering driveways. Lac Echo was on the way up.

These support posts were carved in spirals by Walter DaRold, who also liked to carve totem poles.

Helmut Gransow painted these shutters in a European style called bauernmalerei, *a form of peasant folk art.*

A door carved by Walter DaRold. The dark brown logs, the rococo carving, and the ceiling panels painted by Helmut Gransow combine to make these Lac Echo cottages unique.

As this picture shows, logs don't have to be of immense girth, or even retain the natural color so many people strive for, in order to look good. These logs are made of what many builders would consider "junk" trees: relatively small spruce and balsam. But they do seem to work in these cottages. Even the dark brown paint (painted logs are a distinct rarity) provides a rich, warm, even ancient atmosphere that enhances the antique decor.

There is some controversy about the desirability of painting the ends of logs, as it may inhibit the flow of moisture out of them. Nevertheless, the style is popular at Lac Echo and adds a festive element of color that loggies often lack.

As DaRold's work became known, he received more commissions to carve. But they were usually open-ended commissions because DaRold carved what *he* wanted. He was something of a character — crusty on the outside but warm and creative to the few who knew him. A mechanical engineer until he was forty-two, and with no formal training, he carved spiral-curving posts, fanciful doorways and — his specialty — mantelpieces with the bark stripped off (it would only rot) and then carved to look as if the bark was back on. Although he was heavily influenced by the art of West Coast native peoples, his real strength was his love of and feeling for wood. DaRold worked *with* the wood to bring out the details of knots and grain.

Another of his specialties was making rustic furniture to go with the cabins. His genius was found in the respect he showed for the piece of wood he was transforming: the rough shape, grain and anomalies of a particular slab would be kept and legs or arms added to make the table or chair (see the three-legged campstool on page 91). The piece was always smoothed and rounded off to create a bulky flow. This feeling of bulk and depth was enhanced by multiple coats of varnish. DaRold's respect for wood in its natural state extended to gnarled

Walter DaRold's keen eye and a fondness for revealing the hidden nature of a piece of wood resulted in this whimsical driftwood handrail that resembles a sea serpent, on the lower right. The dark color of most of the approximately thirty Lac Echo cottages — brightened here with red roofing and turquoise trim — comes from a walnut-brown oil-paint.

By the 1960s the lake was attracting more affluent cottagers who began expanding the simple loggies built by George Binns.
This stone addition works well with the original loggie. The new red cedar-shake roof
appears to have been laid right over the old roof.

limbs he found in the woods. Reading fanciful images into the more evocative pieces, he would build them into aspects of the homes he was working on, such as the "sea serpent" handrail pictured on page 95.

By the early 1960s, Helmut Gransow had been asked to add decorative painting to some of the cottages. Gransow had apprenticed for three years as a decorative painter in his native Germany. Now a successful landscape artist who still lives in the area, back in the sixties he was known for his decorative painting. This method of painting designs and scenes on any and all house surfaces, called *bauernmalerei*, has its origins in Bavaria. The craft is what Gransow calls a form of "peasant farm art that people did when they couldn't afford to hang a real painting on the wall, but wanted something decorative."

Inside, these log cottages prove that some things are more than the sum of their parts. They give off a decidedly different and more homey feel than their modern counterparts. There seem to be more books, old books with cloth bindings that have been collected and read by generations of cottagers. The same goes for everything else, from the dishes to the furniture. Everything is old, redolent with use, and evocative of a certain time long past — and that, if you think about it, is an apt description of log homes themselves.

The perfect adornment for a Canadian log wall: a handmade beaver rug.

Logs are alive with tracery and grain. They can be warm to the touch. They are so tactile, in fact, that it's hard to keep your hands off them. Their soft, curving lines and round shapes make a log home the most relaxing of environments.

LIVING WITH LOGS 6

Apart from the obvious historic aspect of owning a real loggie — you are, after all, living in either an authentic antique or an authentic reproduction — there is a particularly sensual aesthetic involved in living in one. Logs are alive with the tracery of grain and shape. They are warm to the touch. They have contour and texture. It is often hard to keep your hands off the wood, especially big wood. People will hug a log post, for example. You can't hug glass or brick. Nor are you inclined to run your hand lovingly over drywall.

Big hewn logs offer a feeling of stability and comfort. Long-log, with its lack of angular form, its soft, curving lines and gentle wood-tones, is the most calming style, but all log buildings share this attribute. Loggies in general are built for people who either have eschewed the fast pace of city life, or who want a retreat from it. The line between city and country is drawn in sharp relief with a log home: everything about it is natural, quiet, even primitive.

Often, the main purpose of the modern log home is to reduce stress. One of the most comforting, cosy images in the world is of a log home muffled by a thick coat of snow, smoke wisping out of the chimney and golden light glowing out of a many-paned window. A lot of owners have obviously chased that dream. Whether a weekend getaway for a high-powered executive, or home sweet home for the truly rural at heart who live there year-round, loggies are as rustic as you can get. No matter what the design, bricks and mortar don't calm you down in and of themselves. Logs *do*.

Part of this comes from their sheer physicality. A well-heated log home literally radiates warmth. The log walls, because of the thousands of tiny air-pockets contained in the wood, hold the heat well. One drawback to these massive walls is that it can take up to two days to heat them. For this reason, a lot of cottagers use computerized heating systems that allow them to turn on the furnace by phone a day or so before they come up, or at least arrange to have a local person do it.

Natural materials, such as this rough stone wall and fieldstone floor, are the most pleasing decor choices for a log home.

But once your log walls have absorbed the heat, they will literally radiate for days, becoming warm, seeming almost alive to the touch.

Then there is the smell. On hot summer days, or when the wood stove has warmed the house, logs tend to give off an aroma distinctive to the wood. The sharp, unmistakable scent of cedar, for example, is released by heat for as long as the building stands. And pine gum, sometimes seen bubbling out of a crack or check, constantly releases a fresh, woodsy aroma throughout the house.

Log buildings also move — a lot! Especially during the first few years if it's a new building, but forever after, because wood contracts when dry and expands when damp. Moisture leaving the log at different rates on opposite sides results in checking — the large, running cracks that are inevitable with big wood. These checks can erupt explosively, like a gunshot, especially when a hot day is followed by a cool night. All of this activity means that log homes are exciting to live in. One owner told us she loved her new loggie because, as she put it, "Our log home seems more alive than other homes we have lived in. It makes noises. It barks at us. It looks different depending on the time of day. It just seems to have more personality."

A nicely crafted way of dealing with a structural problem: As the building settles due to shrinkage, these notches can be loosened to lower the stairs.

The natural materials of granite countertops and a stone oven-surround make this modern kitchen fit comfortably with its log-building roots. The counter stools are made of old milk-cans and tractor seats.

This Quebec builder produces some of the most exciting examples of new directions in log building. His approach is to make everything that is not a log stand out — from the structural members to the trim. The effect is exaggerated by staining the logs themselves, in this case, a soft white by using a clear interior stain with some white paint added.

The builder had some fun here with the interior logs, carving elaborate, multilayered beam-holders and countertops. This builder uses everything from chainsaw oil to saltwater to color and condition the wood.

Log homes are more alive than most habitats. Because the logs shrink (particularly in the round-log style), the walls tend to come down over the windows and doors — and anything else that is stationary. In this picture, a ceiling is making its relentless descent to meet the tops of the cupboards. If built by experts, they will meet perfectly.

This aliveness can also become a problem, however. The most dramatic example of moisture leaving a log is shrinkage, especially in green, undried wood. The long-log construction method doesn't hew the sap-wood layer off, and this is the area where most of the shrinkage occurs (a hewn log is almost all made up of the more stable heartwood). A log can shrink anywhere from one quarter of an inch to one inch over the first two years. This can cause a long-log wall to shrink from four to six inches in total (a hewn wall will shrink two inches at the most). This means that the walls and the roof will slowly come down over the windows and doors.

The idea of your *house* descending like a glacier around you is a startling concept. But it's surprisingly easy to deal with if you know what you're doing. As roof and walls float down with the logs, hollow areas over the windows and doors allow them to settle up into the wall as it comes down. The actual window and door frames are nailed to two-by-four boards (called splines) that are slotted into the sides of openings cut in the log walls. Floating fascia-boards solve any trim problems. On the inside, anything attached to the walls — such as cupboards for instance — will also settle. Allowances have to be made. New log-

Unlike conventional homes, log buildings have exposed ceiling-beams. More than anything else, these beams and joists exemplify the complete functionality of this kind of building method. Not only do the beams hold up the ceiling, they also provide a perfect place for hanging baskets, herbs and dried flowers.

home owners spend a lot of time anxiously watching as the bottom of the ceiling comes down inexorably to meet the top of a line of cupboards that have been hung (or so they hope) low enough to accommodate the settling.

For this and other reasons, log homes aren't exactly low maintenance. For example, some builders put bolts and wingnuts into the bottom of the door or wall posts in order to control the settling. These have to be loosened periodically. The owner can do it easily, but some builders will make the rounds of the homes they have built and do it themselves.

The two dark marks on the wall over the china cabinet were made by a deer sharpening its antlers on the log when it was a tree in the forest. Seeing it as found art with an interesting history, the builder placed it in a prominent location.

A fireplace made from the stone that was blasted out to make room for the basement separates the kitchen from the living room. To avoid unsightly heating ducts, they used forced air to heat the first floor and electric baseboard heaters on the second floor. Some owners hide their stereos and other high-tech toys in armoires, and even put the refrigerator in the basement in order to not spoil the rustic feeling of their log homes.

This handmade loggie was built in 1938. The worn cedar shakes and the Virginia Creeper that grows from the chimney to the eaves make the whole house seem like a living thing. Eschewing the more modern, acrylic chinking products, these owners prefer to pull out the old chinking and rechink with mortar every twenty years or so.

Chinking has to be constantly monitored to make sure no water is getting in behind it. Long-log (scribed) walls should be checked to see that wind is not getting through. If it is, they should be caulked. The same goes for inspecting the walls in general — water settling into checks, crevices or joints can promote wood rot. Wood-boring insects are also a problem, as is dry rot and mildew. These are not serious problems if you stay on top of them, but logs are organic and therefore prone to innumerable natural processes.

The sheer physical size of the logs demands that other architectural elements be in proportion. This general "bigger is better" rule of thumb applies to the interior as well. Giant wrought-iron chandeliers — something thick, rough and very fifteenth century — are perfect for those high, vaulted ceilings. Big, slab coffee-tables look great in a log home, especially in front of a large stone fireplace.

Another decorative motif that fits perfectly with log homes is hewing. The surfaces of log and beam are a perfect medium for the hewer's axe. Worked surfaces are everywhere in some log homes: lintels, ceiling beams, mantels, stairway banisters and even spindles take on a beautifully rough texture. This pull of the primitive is evident in animal skins and

This curved railing is another product of the found-art school of log building. The rough-and-ready spindles, which are drawknifed branches, are a Western approach. Back East they would probably be milled smooth and regular.

A jumble of contrasting styles enlivens this log antique store. Log homes need a lot of color, and even the conflicting styles of a Navaho blanket and a Lenin rug work together here.

buffalo heads, but more subtle touches include primitive art and rough-and-ready antiques — a good example is a harvest table with initials carved on it. A most important element is color — color, color, and more color. Don't use too many earth tones. The endless vista of wood tones can become monotonous, but wood walls and floors make a fine background for colorful artwork and rugs — extravagant kilims and Navaho blankets work particularly well. Painted drywall interior walls are also suitable, as are ceramic and slate floors and granite countertops. And quilts are perfect, not only on beds, but draped over loft railings and chairs. There is even a "log cabin" quilt, which honors hearth and home. The distinctive pattern consists of long rectangles (the logs of the home), getting smaller as they converge toward a red center (the hearth).

What also goes well in a log home are handmade items. Something with a built-in sense of history, like an arrowback chair, a brass kerosene lamp, or a copper frying-pan or tin candle-holder hanging on the wall, adds a wonderful finishing touch (see opposite). And those hewn ceiling-beams cry out for dried flowers and garlands of garlic and herbs. Woven baskets are also at home

Old toys and kerosene lamps evoke the past.

The elements of this staircase are big and chunky, the kind of proportions that fit in well with a log home. Finding just the right kind of curved branch to make a banister or porch rail has some builders scouring the woods.

Silver salvers bunched on a pine wall.

here. Even a collection of antique pewter salvers will glow brightly against mellow-brown pine walls (see photo above).

Another integral part of a log home is the fireplace or wood stove. You almost *have* to have one. The stone of a fireplace or stove and the fire that crackles within are elemental. There is something so comforting about warming up in front of a roaring fire, something that is a big part of the comfort of a loggie. Who imagines curling up by a hot-air register, or warming the hands in front of a cosy baseboard heater? One caveat: wood heat is dry heat. The most interesting way to alleviate this problem we have seen is a cast-aluminum steamer in the shape of a log cabin. When filled with water and placed on top of your wood stove, steam comes out of its chimney to humidify the house.

As with interiors, the exterior landscaping of a log home benefits from the use of natural materials, such as the rock used here. And though any kind of tree is suitable, coniferous trees and shrubs seem to blend in best.

If you follow the dictum that "a log home should look like it grew up out of the ground," your home will always look as if it belongs in its environment. In fact, a well-designed long-log home manages to capture the harmonious relationship between the inside and the outside by minimizing the differences. Lots of glass to let the outside in and maximize the view of a lake or a forest is a must. Natural materials and objects that have at least a touch of the wild in them are the ones that work best on the inside — houseplants, driftwood, granite, wool and birds' eggs are some examples. The elements of wood, fire, water and stone work toward achieving a unity that many in the modern world have lost touch with. It is this pull toward the simple and the natural that causes people to become positively obsessed with log homes.

As for landscaping, the same rules that apply to other homes generally apply to loggies. One exception is that making the landscaping too precise and overcivilized can strike a discordant note. The English garden approach of controlled chaos works best, as do big plantings — they keep the look large, in proportion with the size of the logs. Large expanses of bare lawn don't seem to work with loggies. If you have concrete from the foundation showing, by all

The log motif is continued here with a log bird-feeder, proving that this building method can be delicate as well as massive.

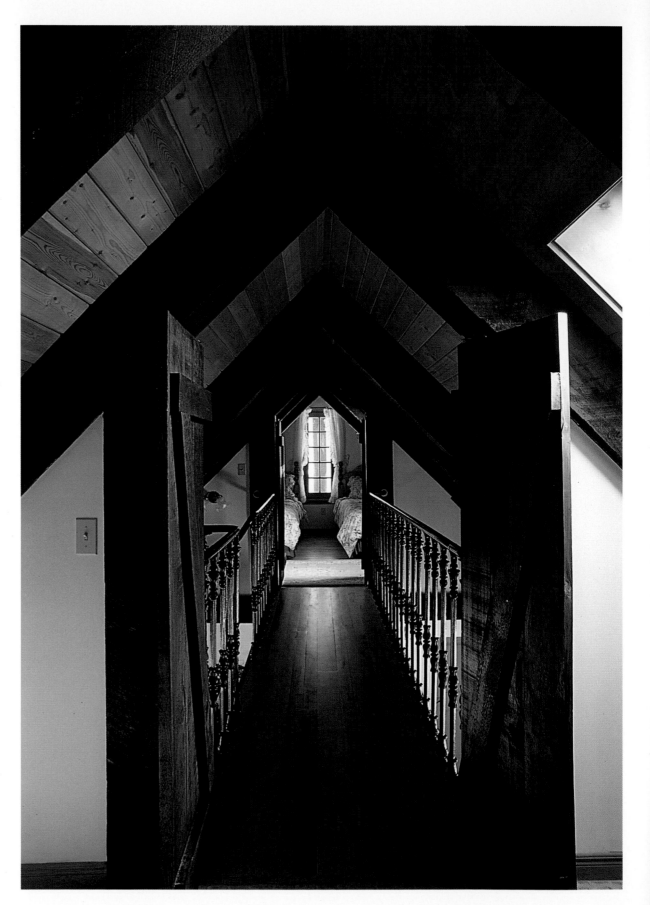

This untraditional log cottage has two small third-floor bedrooms with a connecting passage that looks down to the first floor.

means cover it up with evergreen bushes. Any kind of tree is acceptable around the house, but we have always preferred coniferous over deciduous when it comes to logs, perhaps because the logs themselves are evergreens. Fieldstone looks great with old logs, but new brick doesn't always work.

These decorating and design rules are meant to be broken of course, especially by those intrepid souls who live in log homes and are, by definition, individualistic and creative. Besides, decorating is only about details, while log building is really about the larger issues of peace and quiet, naturalness, and a certain control over your life. For many of us, living in a handcrafted home of big wood is an aesthetically pleasing way of gaining back some of what we have lost to modern life. If you have achieved that kind of peace, enjoy it. Throw another log on the fire, watch the snow come down and admire your logs. If you haven't — well, you can always dream.

A collection of sleigh bells on a rough barnboard wall.

Although usually no longer the main source of heat, a fire in the hearth bestows both physical and emotional warmth.
It is the heart of a log home, giving all who draw near it a focus for their dreams.